WINNING MOVES

Raymond Keene

Collier Books
Macmillan Publishing Company
New York

Maxwell Macmillan Canada
Toronto

Collier Books
Macmillan Publishing
Company
866 Third Avenue
New York, NY 10022

Maxwell Macmillan Canada, Inc.
1200 Eglinton Avenue East
Suite 200
Don Mills, Ontario M3C 3N1

Macmillan Publishing Company is part of the Maxwell
Communication Group of Companies.

Library of Congress Cataloging-in-Publication Data

Raymond, Keene D.
    Winning moves / Raymond Keene.
            p.   cm.
    ISBN 0-02-028702-X
    1. Chess. I. Title.
GV 1449.5.K44 1991
794.1'2--dc20   91-3589
                                                    CIP
Macmillan books are available at special discounts for
bulk purchases for sales promotions, premiums, fund-
raising or educational use. For details, contact:

        Special Sales Director
        Macmillan Publishing Company
        866 Third Avenue
        New York, NY 10022

First Collier Books Edition 1991

10 9 8 7 6 5 4 3 2 1

Printed in Great Britain

Contents

Notation		4
Introduction		6
Scoring System		8
1	Problems 1 - 20	9
2	Problems 21 - 40	17
3	Problems 41 - 60	25
4	Problems 61 - 80	33
5	Problems 81 - 100	41
6	Problems 101 - 120	49
7	Problems 121 - 140	57
8	Problems 141 - 160	65
9	Problems 161 - 180	73
10	Problems 181 - 200	81
11	Problems 201 - 220	89
12	Problems 221 - 240	97
Scorechart		105

Notation

The moves contained in this book are given in what is known as 'Figurine Algebraic Notation'. This somewhat complicated sounding term actually describes a very simple way of writing down the moves. Readers familiar with the system can jump ahead to the positions themselves, but those who are comparatively new to the game or who have only learned the older English Descriptive notation will find what follows helpful. It is assumed that the reader knows how to play chess.

Each piece is represented by a symbol, called a 'Figurine', as follows:

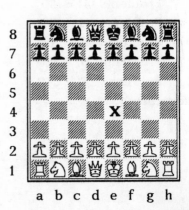

Pawn	♙
Knight	♘
Bishop	♗
Rook	♖
Queen	♕
King	♔

The squares on the chessboard are described by a letter and a number (see diagram). For instance the square marked with a cross is called 'e4'.

To write down a move, first of all a figurine is given, followed by the square to which that piece moves. Thus in the diagram, '1 ♘f3' means that on White's first move he has moved his knight from g1 to f3. Occasionally, more than one similar piece can go to a given square. In such cases, information is also given about the departure square, e.g. '8 ♖ad1' indicates that the white rook standing on the a-file (at a1) moves to d1.

Pawn moves omit the figurine. '1 ... d5' therefore means that Black moves the pawn on d7 to d5. The three dots indicate that this was a move by Black.

Captures are indicated by a 'x' symbol; for instance '17 ♗xg7' indicates that White captured something on g7 with a bishop on move 17.

Castling on the kingside is indicated by 0-0, and on the queenside by 0-0-0.

En passant pawn captures are given as though the captured pawn had moved only one square. For instance, if Black moves a pawn from f7 - f5, next to a white pawn at g5, which then captures the f-pawn, the move is given as 'gxf6', i.e. exactly as if Black had moved the f-pawn to f6 instead of f5.

Various other symbols are used:

+	Check
!	Strong move
!!	Brilliant move
?	Bad move
??	Blunder
!?	Interesting move
?!	Dubious move

Other, more abstruse, symbols are used in many chess books, but not here.

Introduction

This book is based on the Winning Move puzzles which appear every day in *The Times*, and for which every week three chess computers are offered as prizes for correct solutions. The positions may simply be enjoyed for the intellectual challenge that they offer, but they may also serve as a tool for sharpening the tactical ability of the reader, thus improving his or her ability to spot winning moves in actual play. Finally, the puzzles in this book have been so constructed so as to offer the reader a progressive grading system both for each chapter and for the book as a whole. Every position offers points to be scored depending on the speed of solving the problem ranging from five to one. At the end of each chapter the reader will be offered the opportunity to add up the points scored and assess his or her level of strength. It is to be hoped that this level will improve as the reader becomes more experienced by delving further into the book. By adding up the points scored in each chapter and consulting the final table at the end of this book the reader will gain a good overall perspective of the general playing standard attained. The points scored indicate level of strength in category of player (grandmaster, master, expert etc) and also give a parallel indication in international and British rating figures.

The Times Winning Move puzzle has helped *The Times* to gain the largest circulation of readers amongst chessplayers. Each year Lloyds Bank issues a prize chess puzzle which they request all papers with chess columns to publish. The reader response rate for this is widely accepted as the most accurate barometer of which newspapers are being most popularly read for chess. In 1990 Lloyds Bank officials who run the competition announced that *The Times* had won the award for the greatest reader response. Not only was the number of *The Times* readers that replied to what was, in fact, an extremely difficult chess puzzle, an absolute record in the entire history of the competition, the response from *The Times* readers also exceeded the total number of entries combined from *The Independent, The Daily Telegraph, The Sunday Times, The Financial Times* and the now sadly defunct *Sunday Correspondent*. The top scores in descending order were:

Publication	Reader Response
1 *The Times*	545
2 *Mail on Sunday*	395
3 *The Guardian*	296
4 *The Daily Telegraph*	222
5 *The Evening Standard*	96
6 *The Sunday Times*	82
7 *The Financial Times*	80
8 *The Independent*	72
9 *The Sunday Correspondent*	54

Good luck with the solving.

Raymond Keene.

Scoring System

If readers wish to keep a record of their ability to solve the positions, they should score as follows:

A correct solution in one minute or less: 5 points
A correct solution in two to five minutes: 4 points
A correct solution in six to ten minutes: 3 points
A correct solution in eleven to twenty minutes: 2 points
A correct solution in more than twenty minutes: 1 points

Totals for each chapter:

100 points	Grandmaster
90+ points	International Master
80+ points	Master
70+ points	Expert
60+ points	Strong County Player
50+ points	League Player
40+ points	Club Player
30+ points	Enthusiastic Amateur
20+ points	Social Player
less than 20 points	Read *The Times* every day for regular practice.

A scorechart is supplied on pages 106 - 111 for readers to record their scores.

Chapter One

1) This position occurred in the game Nemet – Klinger, Biel 1989. Black to play. What is his winning move?

2) In this position from the game Majzik – Szellosi, Budapest 1989, Black to play wins.

3) In this position, from the game Zsu. Polgar – Arnason, Budapest 1989, what is Black's winning move?

4) This is a variation from the game Sher – Smagin, from the Foreign & Colonial Hastings Masters 1990. What is Black's winning move?

5) This position is a variation from the game Konci – Golombek, Varna Olympiad 1962. How can White take advantage of his aggressive position on the kingside?

6) This position is from the game Farago – Conquest, Foreign & Colonial Hastings Masters 1990. White to play wins.

7) In this position from the game Kaidanov – Lane, Foreign & Colonial Hastings Masters 1990, how does White force a decisive gain of material?

8) This position is from the game Gallagher – Sher, Foreign & Colonial Hastings Masters 1990.
Can you see how White broke down the black defences?

9) This position is from Westerinen – Loikkanen, Finnish Championship 1963. Black has terrible threats on the queenside, but it is White's move. How can he get in first?

10) This position is taken from the game Friedrich – Bantleon, Hanover 1967. White could recapture a piece with 1 ♗xd7, but he has something much stronger. Can you find it?

11) Michael Basman is one of England's most creative International Masters, well-known for his liking of un-orthodox opening systems. In this position from the game Basman – Balshan, played in Israel 1981, how did White force a quick win?

12) This position is from the game Zeck – Travin, Leningrad 1933. How does Black win? There are two possible solutions to this position. Can you spot them both?

13) Grandmaster Daniel King, of Richmond, had an excellent result in the 1989 Grandmasters Association Open.
In this position from the game King – Krasenkov, can you see how he won quickly?

14) Gata Kamsky was one of the USSR's most promising young players until his defection to the USA. In the 1989 Palma de Mallorca tournament he finished equal second, ahead of a number of World class players. In this position from Milos – Kamsky he spotted a chance. to win. How did he continue?

15) This problem is a possible variation from the game Speelman - Cardon, Brussels 1990. In this position, White has just injudiciously captured a black pawn on d5 with his knight. How can Black exploit this lapse?

16) This position is from a game where I played White against the Novag Super VIP chess computer. How does White win quickly?

17) This position is taken from the game Donner - Hubner, Busum 1968. White is two pawns up, but his rook is pinned. How can Black exploit this?

18) This problem is from the game Lungwitz – Lohsse, Volklingen 1970. Can you see how Black can win immediately?

19) This position is taken from the game Carlsson – Eberlein, Biel 1979. White to play and win.

20) This problem is from the game Troyanska – Jovanovic, Oberhausen 1966. Can you see how Black wins immediately?

Chapter One

Solutions

1)   1 ... ♛xf3! 2 gxf3 ♝xf3+ 3 ♔g1 d3+ 4 ♔f1 dxe2+ winning the white queen.

2)   1 ... ♛xf2+! 2 ♔xf2 ♞g4+ 3 ♔e2 ♖f2 mate.

3)   1 ... ♖xc3! 2 ♛xc3 ♞e4 wins material.

4)   1 ... ♖h1+! 2 ♔xh1 ♛xh3+ 3 ♔g1 ♛g2 mate.

5)   1 ♛xh6+! gxh6 2 ♖g8 mate.

6)   White wins material with 1 ♛f6+ ♛xf6 2 exf6+ ♔xf6 3 ♞xf4.

7)   1 ♖xf7! ♖xf7 2 ♝xe6 forces a decisive gain of material. If 1 ... ♔xf7, 2 ♝xe6+ ♛xe6 3 ♖f1+ wins.

8)   1 ♞g4! is decisive, e.g. 1 ... ♝xg3 2 ♞f6+ ♔h8 3 ♞xe8+.

9)   1 ♛xf8+! ♔xf8 2 ♖d8+ ♔e7 3 ♖e8 mate.

10)   1 ♛xc8+! ♝xc8 2 ♖e8 mate.

11)   White forces a quick checkmate with 1 ♖g6+! fxg6 2 ♛h8+! ♔xh8 3 ♖xf8 mate.

12)   1 ... ♛e2+ (1 ... ♖b2+ 2 ♖d2 ♛d1! is also decisive) 2 ♔h3 (if 2 ♔g1 or 2 ♔h1, 2 ... ♖b2 mates) 2 ... ♖h4+! and now either 3 gxh4 ♛f3 mate or 3 ♔xh4 ♛h5 mate.

13)   1 ♛xh7+! ♔xh7 2 ♖h4 mate.

14)   1 ... ♝xe2 and White resigned as 2 ♖xe2 ♛a6 wins a piece.

15)   1 ... ♛xb2+! 2 ♖xb2 ♖h1+ mating.

16)   1 ♖xh7+! ♔xh7 2 ♖h1+ ♖h5 3 ♖xh5+ gxh5 4 ♝e4+ winning the black queen.

17)   1 ... ♖xc5 2 ♛xc5 ♖c8! 3 ♛xb6 ♖xc1+ and 4 ... axb6.

18)   1 ... ♛b2+! 2 ♔xb2 a1(♛) mate.

19)   1 ♖xf8! ♖xf8 2 ♞g6+ hxg6 3 ♛h4+

20)   1 ... ♛h1+! 2 ♝xh1 ♖xh1 mate.

Now turn to page 106 to mark down your scores.

Chapter Two

21) This position is from the game Forbes – Milligan, Blackpool Women's Zonal 1990. How can White conclude the struggle immediately?

22) This position is from the game Geller – Howell, IBM/VISA Open, Reykjavik 1990. White to play and win.

23) This problem is from the game Ivanov – Dimitro, Sofia 1957. White to play and win.

24) This problem is from the game Stahlberg – Becker, Buenos Aires 1944. Can you see how White forces an immediate win?

25) This position is from the game Catalan – Tatai, Dubai 1984. How does Black win with the help of a standard tactical motif?

26) This position is from the game David Taylor – Arthur Freeman, Athenaeum Club Championship 1990. Here White played 1 ♕xh6. What was the opportunity to win material that this move overlooked?

27) This position occurred later in the same game, the decider of the 1990 Championship. How did Black ensure himself of the title from this position?

28) This position is from the game Bird – Gunsberg, London 1887. White to play and win.

29) This position is a possible variation from the game Kumaran – Kennedy, *The Times* British Schools Championship Semi-Final 1990. How can White immediately conclude the game?

30) This problem is from the game King – Keene, London 1982. How can Black finish the game immediately?

31) This position is from the game Karstens – Ulbrich, Swinemunde 1932. Can you spot White's immediate win?

32) This position is from the game Hartlaub – Wahle, Bremen 1923. White to play and win.

33) This problem is from the game Capablanca – Graham, Newcastle 1919. How can White finish the game immediately?

34) This position is from the game Marovic – Piasetski, Toronto 1990. In this position, Black found a clever way to win material. Can you spot it?

35) This position is from the game Razmyslovic – Fisman, USSR 1978. Can you spot White's immediate win?

36) This position is from the game Subaric – Trifunovic, Yugoslavia 1947. How can Black do better than exchanging queens?

37) This problem is from the game Olland – Leussen, Utrecht 1902. How can White exploit the vulnerability of the black back rank to finish the game immediately?

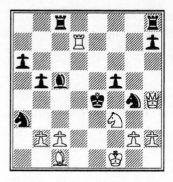

38) This position is from the game Wade – Shoebridge, Australia 1945. White is winning easily on material, but can administer an immediate winning combination. Can you see it?

39) This position is from the game Jagielski – Kohler, Munich 1952. How does White win material with a neat trick?

40) This position is from the game Ekstrom – Bergmann, Sweden 1949. White has a tremendous attack, but his bishop is pinned. How does he continue?

Solutions

21) 1 ♖6h3! traps the black bishop.

22) 1 ♗xb7+! ♖xb7 2 ♖c8+ ♖b8 3 ♕f3+ mating.

23) 1 ♕h8+! ♔xh8 2 ♖xf8 mate.

24) 1 ♕e1+! ♖xe1 2 g3 mate.

25) 1 ... ♖e1+! wins material.

26) 1 ♕xd6 ♖xd6 2 ♗b4 skewers the rooks and thus wins material

27) 1 ... ♕xg3! 2 hxg3 gxh6.

28) 1 ♕xe5+! ♔xe5 2 ♗c3 mate.

29) White wins the black queen with 1 ♖xh7+! ♔xh7 2 ♕xg5.

30) 1 ... ♕xh1+! 2 ♔xh1 ♗xf3++ 3 ♔g1 ♖h1 mate.

31) 1 ♕f6! (threatening 2 ♕g7 mate) 1 ... exf6 2 ♖xe8 mate.

32) 1 ♕g5+! fxg5 2 ♘h6 mate.

33) 1 ♖xc6+! wins the black queen after 1 ... ♕xc6 2 ♘e7+ ♖xe7 3 ♕xc6+.

34) 1 ... ♖xd2! 2 ♕xd2 ♕xe4 forks White's rooks, which cannot both be defended.

35) 1 ♗d5+! cxd5 2 ♕h7 mate.

36) 1 ... ♕xd4! 2 ♗xd4 ♘f3+ 3 ♔f1 ♗b5+ forcing mate.

37) 1 ♕d4! hits the black queen and rook and White meets 1 ... ♕xd4 with 2 ♖e8 mate.

38) 1 ♕e7+! ♗xe7 2 ♖d4 mate.

39) 1 ♗xd7+ ♔xd7 2 0-0-0+ winning the black rook.

40) 1 ♕g8+! ♔xg8 2 ♘e7++ ♔f8 3 ♘xg6 mate.

Now turn to page 106 to mark down your scores.

Chapter Three

41) In this position from the game Vince – Adamski, Budapest 1989, Black to play wins.

42) This position is from the game Cserna – Smyslov, Copenhagen 1986. White to play wins.

43) In this position from the game Geller - Bousla, Erevan 1960, how does White force a quick decision?

44) Ex-World Champion Vasily Smyslov has been a frequent visitor to England, playing in the Lloyds Bank Masters in 1988 and 1989 and Hastings in 1989. In this position from the game Smyslov - Guimard, Mar Del Plata 1962, he demonstrated his quick tactical eye. Can you see how he broke down the Black defences?

45) In this position taken from the game Zilberstein - Veresov, USSR 1952, how can Black win quickly?

46) David Bronstein is one of the strongest players never to have become World Champion. He played Botvinnik for the title in 1951, but Botvinnik drew the match and retained his crown. In this position from the game Keller – Bronstein, Moscow 1956, Black seized the chance to finish off the game with a tactical coup.

47) This position is from the game Chouta – Choutei, Bucharest 1953. How does White deal with the black threats?

48) This position is taken from the game Dubinsky – Bikhovsky, Moscow 1968 How does Black force a win?

49) This position is from the correspondence game Popov - Angelov, played in 1960. Can you see how White forced checkmate?

50) This position is from the game Teschner - Portisch, Monaco 1969. In this position Black played 1 ... ♛a6? and a draw was soon agreed. What did he miss?

51) This position is taken from the game Spassky - Larsen, Palma de Mallorca 1969. How does White force a win?

52) This position is from the game Sakharov - Cherepkov, Alma-Ata 1969. White's bishops are pointing aggressively at the black kingside. How can he capitalise on this?

53) This position is taken from the game Smirnov - Yeletsnov, USSR 1969. How does Black force a quick win?

54) This position is from the game Efimov - Djuric, Sibenik 1989. How can White force a decisive gain of material?

55) This position is from the the game Kichniev - Damljanovic, Sibenik 1989. Both queens are under attack. How can White resolve the situation in his favour?

56) This position is from the game Pape - Stanke, Wernogerode 1980. How can White deal with the threats to his kingside?

57) This position is taken from the game Popov - Ajanski, Plovdiv 1980. How can White exploit his passed pawn in dramatic fashion?

58) This position is from the game Reshevsky – Ivanovic, Skopje 1976. How can Black break through on the king-side?

59) This position is from the game Sinkovic – Molnar, Sopron 1976. Can you see how Black forces a quick mate?

60) This problem is from the game Barriera – Belkadi, Siegen 1970. How can Black exploit the retarded development of White's queen-side?

Solutions

41) 1 ... ♘f3+! 2 gxf3 ♗xe2! 3 ♕xe2 ♕g6+ 4 ♔h1 ♕h5.

42) White wins material with 1 ♕d6! ♘a6 (1 ... ♖f8 2 ♗h7+!) 2 ♖xa7! and Black has no good reply.

43) 1 exf6! ♕xa3 2 ♗xh7+ ♔xh7 3 ♕h5+ ♔g8 4 ♕g5 g6 5 ♕h6 and mate next move.

44) 1 cxb6! ♖e1+ 2 ♖xe1 ♕xb5 3 bxa7 ♕c6 4 ♖b1 ♔h7 5 ♖b8.

45) 1 ... ♕xg2+ 2 ♕xg2 ♗e3 mate.

46) 1 ... ♘5f4+! wins after 2 gxf4 ♖g1+ or 2 ♔f2 ♘h3+.

47) 1 ♖g5! ♕xf6 (1 ... ♕xg5 2 ♘xf7 mate) 2 ♕d4! ♕xd4 3 ♘xf7 mate.

48) 1 ... ♕xd1+! 2 ♗xd1 ♖xd1+ 3 ♔c2 ♖c1+! and 4 ... ♘d3+ wins the white queen, or 3 ♔a2 ♘d3! with the decisive threat of 4 ... ♘b4 mating.

49) White forces mate with 1 ♖g3+ ♔f8 2 ♖d7! ♗xd7 3 ♕d6+ ♖e7 4 ♕h6+ ♔e8 5 ♖g8.

50) 1 ... ♕f2! wins, e.g. 2 ♖xf2 ♖e1 mate or 2 ♘g3 ♕e1+!

51) 1 ♕c8+ ♔h7 2 ♕xe6! fxe6 3 f7 winning.

52) 1 ♗xh7+! ♔xh7 2 ♖xd6 ♗xd6 3 ♖h4+ ♔g8 4 ♖h8+! ♔xh8 5 ♕h6+ ♔g8 6 ♕xg7 mate.

53) 1 ... e2+! 2 ♗xe2 ♕d4+! 3 ♕xd4 (3 ♔e1 or 3 ♔c2 3 ... ♖xc3) 3 ... ♖c1 mate.

54) 1 ♖xb7! ♖xb7 2 ♖c8+ ♔f7 3 ♗e8+ picks up the queen.

55) 1 ♕xc8! wins material, as 1 ... ♕xc8 allows 2 ♘f6+ ♔h8 3 ♖h7 mate.

56) 1 ♕xf7+ ♔xf7 2 ♗d5 mate.

57) 1 ♕f6! ♗xf6 2 exf6 and the h-pawn promotes.

58) 1 ... ♕xh2+! 2 ♔xh2 ♖h4+ 3 ♔g1 ♘g3 and 4 ... ♖h1 mate.

59) 1 ... ♕h4+ 2 gxh4 ♖c3+ forcing mate.

60) 1 ... ♗c5! 2 ♕xc5 ♕e1 mate.

Now turn to page 107 to mark down your scores.

Chapter Four

61) This position is from the game Unzicker - Dankert, Munich 1979. Black to play and win.

62) This position is from the game Bronstein - Goldenov, Kiev 1944. Can White do better than exchanging queens?

63) In this position, from the game Medina - Tal, Palma de Mallorca 1967, can you see how Tal spotted an opportunity to cash in on his dangerous h-pawn?

64) This position is from the game Nikolic - Maric, Vrnjacka Banja 1965. Black to play and win.

65) This position is taken from the game Larsen E - Erlandsson, Sweden 1966. How does Black exploit his tremendous kingside initiative?

66) In this position from the game Minic – Honfi, Vrnjacka Banja 1966, black's king lacks an escape square from the back rank. Can you see how White can take advantage of this?

67) This position is from the game Bernstein – Kotov, Groningen 1946. The white rooks have invaded the black position. How can he administer the coup de grace?

68) This position is from the game Popova – Kasinova, USSR 1974. Can you see how White finishes off his king-side attack?

69) This position is taken from the game Lesiege - Huber, Canada 1989. How does White exploit his kingside initiative?

70) In this position from the game Arkell - Kosten, Hastings 1990, White has just carelessly retreated his rook from c7 to c2. Why was this a mistake?

71) This position is from the game Piket - Martinovic, Groningen 1989. White to play and win.

72) This problem is from the game Andersson S - Knutsson, Stockholm 1974. Can you see how Black wins immediately?

73) This position is from the game Polvine - Kreitchik, USSR 1961. How can Black win immediately?

74) This position is taken from the game Molinari - Cabral, Uruguay 1943. How does Black finish off his kingside attack?

75) This position is from the game Seleznov – Panov, USSR 1929. How can Black profit from his dangerously placed pieces?

76) This position is from the game Ivkov – Portisch, Bled 1961. The black king is in a tight corner. Can you see how White exploits this?

77) This position is from the game Georgadze – Kuindzi, USSR 1973. Black to play and win.

78) This position is from the game Dietrich – Bauer, Austria 1967. Black forces the win with a surprising maneouvre. Can you spot it?

79) Here is a problem from the game Kudari – Larsen, Ottawa 1970. How can Black finish the game immediately?

80) This position is from the game Skuratov – Svedcikov, USSR 1972. How can White capitalize most efficiently on his passed pawns?

Solutions

61) 1 ... ♛g3+! 2 ♔h1 (2 ♖xg3 hxg3+ 3 ♔h1 ♞f2 mate) 2 ... ♛xf3 3 gxf3 ♞f2+ wins material.

62) 1 ♖c8! ♖xc8 2 ♖xc8 ♛xc8 3 ♛e7 mate.

63) 1 ... ♛xf3+ 2 ♔xf3 ♞e3! and the pawn will promote.

64) 1 ... ♗g3! wins, as 2 ♖xf6 allows 2 ... ♖e1 mate.

65) 1 ... ♛h3! 2 gxh3 ♗f3! and 3 ... ♞xh3 mate is unstoppable.

66) 1 ♛a7! causes an overload in the black position. Black is without a reasonable reply.

67) 1 ♖h8+ ♔g6 2 f5+ exf5 3 ♛xh6+! gxh6 4 ♖ag8 mate.

68) 1 ♛xh7+! ♔xh7 2 ♖h1+ ♔g8 3 ♖h8+ ♔f7 4 ♞g5 mate.

69) 1 ♞f8+! ♞xf8 2 ♛h5 mate. If 1 ... ♔h6 or 1 ... ♔h8, then 2 ♛h3 is mate.

70) 1 ... ♛c7! and the white rook is caught in the crossfire.

71) 1 d8(♛)+! ♛xd8 2 ♛xf7 mate.

72) 1 ... ♛d1+! 2 ♔xd1 ♗g4++ and 3 ... ♖d1 mate.

73) 1 ... ♛xh2+! 2 ♔xh2 ♞g4+ 3 ♔h1 ♖h3+ 4 gxh3 ♖h2 mate.

74) 1 ... ♗g1+! 2 ♛xg1 (2 ♔xg1 ♛xg3+) 2 ... ♞g4+! 3 hxg4 ♛h6+ 4 ♗h4 ♛xh4 mate.

75) 1 ... ♖xe2! 2 ♖xe2 ♗xg2+! and 3 ... ♛b1+ mating.

76) 1 ♖c6+! ♗xc6 2 ♞c5+ ♔a5 3 ♗c7 mate.

77) 1 ... ♛f2+! 2 ♛xf2 ♖h5+! 3 ♗xh5 g5 mate.

78) 1 ... ♞h1+! 2 ♖xh1 ♖df2 and there is no defence against 3 ... ♖8f3 mate.

79) 1 ... ♖f2! 2 ♖xf2 (2 ♗xf2 ♛g2 mate) 2 ... exf2+ 3 ♔xf2 ♖f8+ 4 ♔f3 ♛e3+.

80) 1 ♖h5! ♖xh5 2 fxe7 and the white pawn queens.

Now turn to page 107 to mark down your scores.

Chapter Five

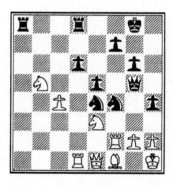

81) In this position from the game Ponomarev – Pugatjev, USSR 1989, Black to play wins.

82) In this position from the game Gejzerskij – Masjtjbic, USSR 1989, Black to play wins.

83) This position is from the game Gallagher – Lane, Foreign & Colonial Hastings Masters 1990, Despite the reduced material, White forced a quick win. Can you see how?

84) This position is from the game Vasiukov – Pribyl, Hungary 1977. White has a very active position and the black king is stuck in the centre. Can you see how White can exploit these factors?

85) In this position, from the game Lobazov – Gorniak, Kalinine 1964, Black forced a quick win.

86) In this position, from the game Hallier – Herman, Hamburg 1965, how does White win quickly?

87) This position is from the game Schneider – Federau, Berlin 1979. How can Black win immediately?

88) This position is from the game Benjamin – Dlugy, New York 1988. Can White do better than retreating his knight?

89) This position is from the game Garcia P – van der Wiel, Kastrikjum 1980. How does White exploit the chronic dark square weaknesses in the black kingside?

90) This position is from the game Tal – Olafsson, Las Palmas 1975. The white back rank is very weak – can you see how Black took advantage of this?

91) In this position, from the game Askelof – Svensson, Sweden 1981, can you see how Black exploited the exposed position of the white king?

92) This problem is from the game Siekanski – Stratil, Oakham Junior International 1990. How does White win at once?

93) In this position, from the game Blatny – Ruxton, Oakham Junior International 1990, can you see how White can break through on the queenside?

94) This position is from the game Wolff – Hodgson, WFW/City Of London Corporation International 1990. What is Black's most direct route to victory?

95) This position is a possible variation from the exciting last round game Motwani - Larsen, WFW/ City Of London Corporation International 1990. White is two rooks down, but has a tremendous attacking position. Can you see how he forces the win?

96) This position is from the game Lutikov - Tal, Kiev 1964. How can White exploit his dangerous passed pawn on f7?

97) In this position, from the game Sherzer - Mate, Budapest 1989, White has a brilliant winning coup. Can you spot it?

98) This position is from the game Simagin - Abramov, Moscow 1949. How can White checkmate quickly?

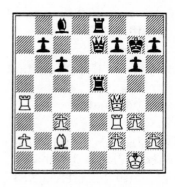

99) This position is from the game Netto - Abente, Peru 1983. Black has a forcing sequence to deliver checkmate. Can you see it?

100) This position is taken from the game Spassov - Kozma, Zinnowitz 1965. White has a tremendous concentration of forces on the kingside. How does he now cash in?

Solutions

81) 1 ... ♞g3+! 2 ♔g1 ♞h3+ 3 gxh3 ♞e2+ 4 ♔h1 ♛g1 mate.
     If 2 hxg3 hxg3, intending ... ♛h4, wins.

82) 1 ... ♛g3! 2 hxg3 ♖h5 mate. Other defences also fail:
     2 ♖xe3 ♖c1+, 2 ♛xe3 ♛xe3 3 ♖xe3 ♖c1+ or 2 ♖d1 ♖h5 3
     h3 ♖xh3+ 4 gxh3 ♛xh3 mate.

83) 1 ♞d7+ ♔a8 2 ♖c5! ♖xd7 3 ♖c8 mate.

84) 1 ♞c7+! ♞xc7 2 ♖xe7+! ♔xe7 3 ♛f6+ ♔e8 4 ♖d8 mate.

85) 1 ... ♖xd3! 2 cxd3 ♛xe4! 3 fxe4 c2 forces a new queen.

86) 1 ♛g3+ ♛xg3 2 ♞e7+! ♞xe7 3 ♗xf7 mate.

87) Black captures the white queen with 1 ... ♛f1+ 2 ♔e3
     ♞f5+! 3 exf5 ♛e1+.

88) 1 ♞e5! leaves no answer to the combined threats of 2
     ♗g5, 2 ♖f7 and 2 ♞g6. If 1 ... ♔d8 2 ♞f7+.

89) 1 ♖xf5! ♖xf5 2 ♛e5+! ♖xe5 3 ♗f6 mate.

90) 1 ... ♛g5! overloads the white queen. If 2 ♛xg5 ♖xe1
     mate, or 2 ♛b4 ♛xe7!

91) 1 ... ♖e1+! 2 ♖xe1 ♛g1+! 3 ♔xg1 ♖xe1 mate.

92) 1 ♛xf7+! ♔xf7 2 ♞xd6+.

93) 1 ♖xb6+! axb6 2 a7+ ♔xa7 (2 ... ♔a8 or 2 ... ♔b7 leads
     to the same after 3 ♛c6+) 3 ♛c7+ ♔a8 4 ♗c6 mate.

94) 1 ... ♛g1+! 2 ♔xf3 (2 ♔h3 ♛h2 mate) 2 ... ♛f1+ 3 ♔e3
     ♛e1+ picks up the white queen.

95) 1 ♗h7++! ♔f8 2 ♛g7+ ♔e8 3 ♞xf6+ ♔d8 4 ♛xd7 mate.

96) 1 ♛xd8! ♖xd8 2 ♖xd7+ ♖xd7 3 f8(♛).

97) 1 ♛g5+! ♗xg5 2 hxg5+ ♔xh5 3 g4 mate.

98) 1 ♖xh6+! ♛xh6 (1 ... ♔xh6 2 ♛h8 mate) 2 ♛e2+ ♔g5 3
     ♛e7+ ♔g4 (3 ... ♔h5 4 ♛h4 mate) 4 f3+ ♔h5 5 ♛h4.

99) 1 ... ♖e1+ 2 ♔g2 ♖g1+! 3 ♔xg1 ♛e1+ 4 ♔g2 ♛f1+! 5 ♔xf1
     ♗h3+ 6 ♔g1 ♖e1 mate.

100) 1 ♖xg7+! ♖xg7 2 ♖e8+ ♔f7 3 ♛xg7+ ♔xe8 4 ♛f8 mate.

Now turn to page 108 to mark down your scores.

Chapter Six

101) This problem is from the game Popov – Novopashin, Munich 1979. Can you see how White wins immediately?

102) In this position, from the game Bohling – Starck, Lipsia 1972, can you see how Black wins immediately?

103) This position is from the game Borisenko – Simagin, Moscow 1955. White is a pawn up but his king is dangerously positioned. How does Black exploit this?

104) This position is from the game Feher – Mate, Budapest 1989. Can you spot White's brilliant winning continuation?

105) This position is from the game Ludolf – Koc, Leningrad 1960. Can you see how White exploits the vulnerable position of the black king?

106) This position is from the game Lundin – Momo, Leipzig 1960. What is the most efficient conclusion to White's attack?

107) This problem is from the game Reti – Tartakower, Vienna 1910. Can you see how White administers a brilliant coup?

108) This position is from Gurevich M – Short, Rotterdam 1990. Nigel has just captured a pawn on f5 with his queen. Can you see what he overlooked?

109) This position is from the game Kochtenko - Lerner, USSR 1962. How does White resolve the problem of his attacked rook?

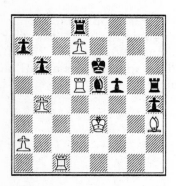

110) This position is from the game Straonttinch - Zauerman, Correspondence 1984. Can you see how White wins immediately?

111) This position is from the game Lasker - Mieses, Leipzig 1889. Can you spot White's brilliant finish?

112) This position is from the game Schmid – Keres, Tel Aviv Olympiad 1964. White to play and win.

113) This position is from the game Schiffers – Tchigorin, Berlin 1897. It is famous as one of the great missed opportunities of chess. Despite his deficit of a queen for a piece, Black has a winning combination, which he overlooked with 1 ... b6? Can you do better?

114) This position is from the game Alden – Nilsson, Sweden 1972. How can Black exploit White's vulnerable back rank?

115) This position is from the game Alapin – Levitsky, St. Petersburg 1911. White blundered here with 1 ♕e8. Can you do better?

116) This position is from the game Engelbert – Hofmann, Schleusingen 1961. Black cannot capture the White queen on account of ♖a8+. What should he do instead, in order to save himself?

117) This position is from the game Suba – Portisch, Thessaloniki 1984. White's development is lacking and his queen is attacked. How can Black immediately exploit these factors?

118) This position is from the game Ostropolski – Ivanovski, USSR 1949. Can you spot White's brilliant winning continuation?

119) This problem is from the game Taimanov – Kuzmin, USSR 1950. Can you see how White forces an immediate win?

120) This position is from the game Miles – Schneider, Philadelphia 1980. White is a piece up, but how can he cope with Black's dangerous pawn on b2?

Chapter Six

Solutions

101) 1 ♕h6+! wins i.e. 1 ... gxh6 2 ♖xb7+ or 1 ... ♔xh6 2 ♖h8.

102) 1 ... ♕f7! 2 ♕xf7 ♖xd1+ and 3 ... ♘xf7.

103) 1 ... f5+! 2 exf6 e.p. (2 ♔h4 ♕h1 mate) 2 ... ♕f5+ 3 ♔h4 ♕h5 mate.

104) 1 ♖c6! ♕xc6 (1 ... ♗e6 2 ♖xe6 leads to the same finish) 2 ♕g7+ ♔h5 3 ♗f3 mate.

105) 1 ♖d8+! ♖xd8 (1 ... ♕xd8 2 ♕e5+) 2 ♕c3+ mating.

106) 1 ♕d8+! ♖xd8 2 ♖e7+ ♔f8 3 ♖fxf7 mate.

107) 1 ♘d8+! ♔xd8 2 ♗g5++ ♔c7 (2 ... ♔e8 3 ♖d8 mate) 3 ♗d8 mate.

108) 1 ♕xh6+! gxh6 2 ♖hxh6 mate.

109) 1 ♕f3! ♕xf3 2 ♖g1+ mating. If 1 ... ♕g6 2 0-0-0 and 3 ♖dg1 will win the queen.

110) 1 ♖c6+! ♔xd5 2 ♗g2 mate.

111) 1 ♕xg6+! ♔xg6 2 ♖g3+ ♔h7 3 ♗d3+ ♔h6 4 ♘f7 mate. If 2 ... ♔h6 3 ♘f7+ ♔h7 4 ♗d3 mate.

112) 1 ♖xf5+! ♔xf5 2 ♕h7+ ♔e5 (or 2 ... ♔f6) 3 ♕h8+ skewering the Black queen.

113) 1 ... ♖h1+! 2 ♘xh1 ♗h2+! 3 ♔xh2 ♖h8+ 4 ♔g3 ♘f5+ 5 ♔g4 (or 5 ♔f4) 5 ... ♖h4 mate.

114) 1 ... ♕c6! wins the rook. If 2 ♕xc6 or 2 ♖xc6 2 ... ♖d1+.

115) 1 ♕xg8+! ♔xg8 2 ♖exg7+ ♔h8 3 ♖g8+ ♔h7 4 ♖2g7 mate.

116) 1 ... ♖b1+ 2 ♔g2 ♘f4+! 3 ♔f3 (3 ♕xf4 ♕xa6 or 3 gxf4 ♕xg4+) 3 ... ♘e6 and Black escapes.

117) 1 ... ♖d1+! creates insoluble problems, e.g. 2 ♖xd1 ♘xb4 or 2 ♔xd1 ♘xc3+!

118) 1 ♕xd7+! ♖xd7 2 ♘c7+ ♖xc7 3 ♖d8 mate.

119) 1 ♕xd8+! ♕xd8 2 ♗xe6 mate.

120) 1 ♘g6! wins. 1 ... b1(♕) 2 ♖h8 mate, or 1 ... fxg6 2 fxg6+ and 3 ♖xf1, preventing the pawn promoting.

Now turn to page 108 to mark down your scores.

Chapter Seven

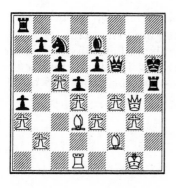

121) This position is from the game Geller - Notaros, Novi Sad 1978, Black is a rook ahead, but White has the chance for a brilliant drawing combination. Can you see it?

122) This position is from the game Berger - Kos, Graz 1882. White to play and win.

123) This position is from the game Reti – Bogolyubov, New York 1924. How does White exploit his pressure on the f-file?

124) This position is from the game Hromadka – Samisch, Piestany 1922. Black has got 'in round the back'. How can he capitalise on his efforts?

125) This problem is from the game Trifunovic – Aaron, Beverwijk 1962. What is the quickest way for White to exploit the light square weaknesses in Black's kingside?

126) This position is from the game Bachtiar – Liang, Indonesia 1961. Black is a piece up but his knight and bishop are attacked. How does he resolve his difficulties?

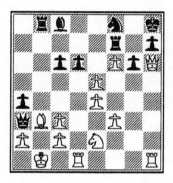

127) This position is from the game Skuja – Rozenberg, Riga 1962. Can you spot White's brilliant mating combination?

128) This position is from the game Hinks – Clifford, City Chess Quickplay 1990. How did Black finish off his opponent with a dazzling combination?

129) This problem is from the game Cevallos - Mohring, Tel Aviv 1964. How can Black win without further ado?

130) This position is from the game Bogomolov - Kozlov, Moscow 1976. How does White capitalise on his concentration of forces on the kingside?

131) This position is from the game Garbett - West, Sydney 1989. The black king is very constricted. Can you see how White exploited this?

132) In this position from the game Onouchko – Avramenko, USSR 1989, Black has a long forcing sequence resulting in mate or win of material. Can you spot it?

133) This position is from the game Akhipkine – Kuznetsov, Kiev 1980. White to play and win.

134) This position is from the game Wallner – Stoppel, Austria 1989. How does Black exploit the white king's dangerous shortage of squares?

135) This position is from the game Polyak - Levin, Kiev 1949. Although Black is a piece up, he seems to be in trouble as his queen and rook are attacked. How did he turn the tables on White?

136) This position is from the game Larson - Englund, Iceland 1942. Black to play and win.

137) This position is from the game Sturua - Nunn, Lloyds Bank Masters, London 1990. White is material ahead, but his pieces are under attack. How can he cope with the threats?

138) This position is from the game Conquest – Kaidanov, Lloyds Bank Masters, London 1990. White to play and win.

139) This problem is from the game Rada – Kostal, Prague 1942. Here White finished matters off with a superb mating combination. Can you see it?

140) This position is from the game Gereben – Komarov, Moscow 1949. Can you spot Black's brilliant winning continuation?

Solutions

121) 1 Qxh5+! Kxh5 2 g4+! Kxg4 (2 ... Kh6 3 g5+ wins the queen) 3 Be2+ with perpetual check on d3, e2 and f1.

122) 1 Qa8+ Kh7 2 Qh8+! Nxh8 3 Rg7 mate.

123) 1 Bf7+ Kh8 2 Be8! wins, e.g. 2 ... Rxe8 3 Qxf8+, 2 ... Bxc5+ 3 Qxc5 Rxe8 4 Rf8+ or 2 ... Be7 3 Qf8+.

124) 1 ... Rd1! wins, as 2 Rxd1 Qxf2+ 3 Kh1 Qg1 is mate.

125) 1 Bg8! threatening 2 Qh7 mate and 2 Rxd8.

126) 1 ... Re2! and if 2 Nxe2 Qe1 mate.

127) 1 Qxf8+ Rxf8 2 Rxh7+ Kxh7 3 Rh1 mate.

128) 1 ... Nf3! 2 Qd1 (2 Bxf3 Qxh2 mate) 2 ... Qxg3! 3 Qg1 (3 hxg3 Nf2 mate) 3 ... Qxh2+! 4 Qxh2 Nf2 mate.

129) 1 ... Rh1+! 2 Kxh1 Bxf2 and 3 ... Rh8+ mating.

130) 1 Qxh7+! Kxh7 2 Bg6! (threatening 3 Rh3+ and 4 Rh8 mate) 2 ... Rxe6 3 Rh3+ Kg8 4 fxe6 and 5 Rh8 mate.

131) 1 Rf7! Qxf7 2 Qxe5+ Rg7 3 hxg7+ Qxg7 4 Rxh7+.

132) 1 ... Rh1+! 2 Kg2 (2 Kxh1 Qh8+ 3 Kg1 Qh2+ 4 Kf1 g2+ 5 Ke2 g1(Q)+) 2 ... Qb2+ 3 Kxg3 Qh2+ 4 Kg4 Qh4 mate.

133) 1 Qh5! gxh5 (1 ... h6 2 Qxh6!) 2 Rg3+ Bg7 3 Rxg7+ Kf8 4 Rxh7 and 5 Rh8 mate.

134) 1 ... Bc4! 2 Qe1 Bc3+! 3 Qxc3 Bf1 mate.

135) 1 ... Rc8! 2 Rxd4 Nxd4 threatening 3 ... Rc1! against which there is no reasonable defence, e.g. 3 Kh1 Ne2!

136) 1 ... Nd1+! 2 Kg1 Nc3! with dual threats of 3 ... Qe3 mate and 3 ... Ba4! trapping the black queen.

137) 1 Rd7! Rxd7 (1 ... Bxe1 2 Qg6+ Kh8 3 Qxe8+ Kh7 4 Qg6+) 2 Qg8+ Kxh6 3 Qg6 mate.

138) 1 Rxg6! fxg6 2 Qxh5+ Kg8 3 Bb3+ Kf8 4 Qh8+.

139) 1 Qg4+! Bxg4 2 Rxh6+! gxh6 3 Bf7 mate.

140) 1 ... Qxh3+! 2 Nxh3 g4 and White will be mated by 3 ... Rxh3 and 4 ... Rh1.

Now turn to page 109 to mark down your score.

Chapter Eight

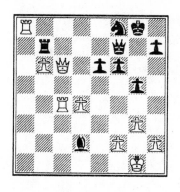

141) This position is from the game Koch - Kogan, Singapore 1990. How can White make the most of his active pieces and dangerous passed pawn?

142) This position is from the game Guigonis - Dussol, Paris 1990. Can you spot Black's winning continuation?

143) This position is from the game Zollner - Velasco, Munich 1934. Black has sacrificed his queen for a tremendous kingside attack. Can you see how he forced checkmate?

144) This position is from the game Lyczynowicz - Szymanski, Poland 1953. Black to play and win.

145) This problem is a possible variation from the game van der Wiel - Piket, Holland 1990. White has just sacrificed his queen to open the g-file to the black king. How can he conclude immediately?

146) This position is from the game Ornstein – Schneider, Sweden 1985. Can you work out how Black forces mate with a checking sequence?

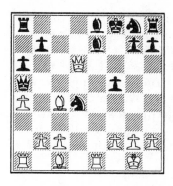

147) This position is from the game Ofstad – Uhlmann, Halle 1963. Can you see White's brilliant winning coup?

148) This position is from the game Kamysev – Sokolsky, USSR 1936. Black to play and win.

149) This problem is from the game Kotronias – King, Watson, Farley & Williams International Challenge, New York 1990. White to play and win.

150) This position is from the game Speelman – Hodgson, in the Watson, Farley & Williams International challenge, New York 1990. In this innocent-looking position White forces immediate resignation. Can you see how?

151) This position is from the game Fishbein – Kotronias, Watson, Farley & Williams International Challenge, New York 1990. Black has just offered a bishop sacrifice on g3. How should white respond?

152) This position is from the game Hodgson – King, Watson, Farley & Williams International Challenge, New York 1990. How did Black terminate proceedings immediately?

153) This position is from the game Alekhine – Schwartz, London 1926. Although White is a rook down, he can win by force. Can you see how?

154) This position is from the game Andruet – Birmingham, Angers 1990. How can White break down the black fortress?

155) This problem is from the game Jacobs - Mannion, Nat West Masters 1987. Can you see White's knock-out blow?

156) This position is from the game Cairou - Cech, Paris 1990. Black has a forcing continuation that leads to checkmate. Can you see it?

157) This position is from the game Saunina - Chekhova, Sochi 1981. How can White force an immediate win?

158) This position is from the game Oberg - Unander, Finland 1983. Black's rook and bishop are both threatened, but he has a beautiful way to resolve the problem. Can you see it?

159) This position is from the game Machulsky - Gurevich, USSR 1977. A quick glance at this position reveals that White has five pieces developed and Black only one, so it is not surprising that White has an immediate forced win. Can you see it?

160) This position is from the game Moiseev - Ilivinsky, Primorsko 1974. Can you see how White powered his way through to the black king?

Solutions

141) 1 Rxf8+! Kxf8 (1 ... Qxf8 2 Qxb7) 2 Qc8+ Kg7 3 Qxb7! Qxb7 4 Rc7+ Qxc7 5 bxc7 and the pawn promotes.

142) 1 ... Rxc3! 2 Qxc3 Qxa2+ 3 Kf1 Bb5+ 4 Ke1 Qe2 mate.

143) 1 ... Nf3+! 2 gxf3 Bxf3 mates, e.g. 3 hxg3 Rh1 or 3 h3 Rxh3 and 4 ... Rh1 mate.

144) 1 ... Qxe5+! 2 Qxe5 h4 3 g4 (otherwise 3 ... Rh1 mate) 3 ... Rf2 mate.

145) 1 Ne7+! Bxe7 2 Rhg1+ mating.

146) 1 ... Nh4+! 2 gxh4 R4d3+ 3 Ke4 (3 Kg2 Bh3+ and 4 ... Rd1+ mating) 3 ... f5+ 4 Kxe5 Re2+ 5 Kf4 Re4 mate.

147) 1 Rxe7! Nxe7 2 Qf6+! gxf6 3 Bh6 mate.

148) 1 ... Qxg4! 2 hxg4 Rh5+! 3 gxh5 Rh4 mate.

149) 1 Qh6! gxh6 2 Nxh6 mate.

150) 1 Bd5! wins, e.g. 1 ... exd5 2 Nxf6+ and 3 Qxe7 or 1 ... Qxd5 2 Rc8! Rxc8 3 Nxf6+ and 4 Nxd5.

151) 1 Qd4+! Qxd4 2 Bxd4+ and 3 fxg3 with an extra piece.

152) 1 ... Rc3! snares the white queen, e.g. 2 Qa1 Rxg3+! and 3 ... Bxa1 with an easy win.

153) 1 Rxc7+ Rxc7 2 bxc7 Re8 3 cxb8(Q)+ Rxb8 4 Be6! and the c-pawn will cost Black his rook.

154) 1 Nxb5! cxb5 2 Qh8+ Bf8 3 Bxb5+ Ke7 4 Qf6 mate.

155) 1 Ng5! hxg5 2 Qh5 mate.

156) 1 ... Qh1+ 2 Ng1 Bxf4 3 Qxf4 Re1+! 4 Kxe1 Qxg1+ 5 Kd2 Qd3 mate.

157) 1 Ng5 Qg6 2 Qxh7+! Qxh7 3 Nxf7 mate.

158) 1 ... Rc1! 2 Rxc1 Bxe3+ and 3 ... Bxc1.

159) 1 Qxe6+! fxe6 2 Bxg6+ Ke7 3 Bg5+ Nf6 4 exf6+ Kd7 5 Ne5 mate.

160) 1 Rxg7+! Bxg7 2 Rxg7+ Kh8 3 Rxg8+! Kxg8 4 Qg6+ Kh8 5 Qg7 mate.

Now turn to page 109 to mark down your score.

Chapter Nine

161) This position is from the game Stratil – Tozer, Oakham Junior International 1990. Black has sacrificed two pawns to open lines on the kingside. How can he make use of them?

162) This position is taken from the game Blatny – Stangl, Oakham Junior International 1990. Can White exploit the isolated position of the black queen?

163) This problem is from the game Fuller – Steedman, Chester 1979. Can you spot White's win?

164) In this position, from the game between two grandmasters, Hodgson and Chandler, Watson, Farley & Williams International 1990, how does White finish off his kingside attack?

165) This problem is from the game Tukmakov – Norwood, Reykjavik 1990. Can you see how White wins immediately?

166) In this position, from the game Carton - Adams, Blackpool Zonal 1990, can you see how Black wins immediately?

167) This position is from the game Suba - Davies, Blackpool Zonal 1990 . Can you see how White immediately terminates the Black resistance?

168) This position is from the game Milligan - Jackson, Blackpool Women's Zonal 1990. How does Black exploit her dangerous passed pawns?

Chapter Nine

169) This position is from the game Dedes - Makropoulos, Greece 1990. How can White break the pin on his knight?

170) This position is from the game Polyak - Kholmov, Riga 1954. White has a promising attack but his back rank is weak (e.g. 1 ♖xe7+? ♕xe7 2 ♘xe7 ♖a1+). How did he solve this problem?

171) This position is from the game Fedder - Westerinen, Roskilde 1978. How can Black win immediately?

172) This position is from the game Padevski – Belkadi, Varna 1962. Black to play and win.

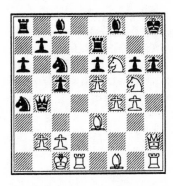

173) This position is from the game Braga – Rossetto, Argentina 1980. Can you see how White delivered mate with a long forcing manoeuvre?

174) This position is from the game Friker – de Vita, Catanzaro 1979. White to play and win.

175) This problem is from the game Bates – Fearn, *The Times* British Schools Championship Final. Can you spot White's immediate win?

176) This position is from the game Florence – Piper, *The Times* British Schools Championship Semi-Finals 1990. How can Black force an immediate win?

177) This position is from the game Petrov – Chimansky, Warsaw 1847. White to play and win.

178) This position is from the game Martinik - Dobosh, France 1973. How does Black capitalise on White's lack of development?

179) This problem is from the game Saemisch - Reimann, Bremen 1927. How does White conclude proceedings in dramatic fashion?

180) This position is from the game Bennini - Reggio, Rome 1911. Can you spot White's elegant winning combination?

Solutions

161) 1 ... ♕xg5! wins a piece as 2 ♘xg5 allows 2 ... ♗xf2 mate, and 2 ♘xc6 is met by 2 ... ♖xf4.

162) 1 ♘a4! traps the black queen. After 1 ... ♘xe4 2 ♕d3 ♕b4 3 ♕xe4, White has won a piece.

163) 1 ♕g7+! ♖xg7 2 fxg7 mate.

164) 1 ♘f6+ ♖xf6 2 ♕xe8+

165) 1 ♖d7+! ♕xd7+ 2 ♘xe5+ costs Black his queen.

166) 1 ... ♖xf1+! 2 ♖xf1 ♕e3.

167) 1 ♘f6+! ♗xf6 2 ♖xe7 ♗xe7 3 ♕xf7+ and 4 ♕xe7.

168) 1 ... c4! (not 1 ... c2? 2 ♘d3!) leaves White helpless, e.g. 2 ♔e2 c2 3 ♗b2 a3 4 ♗c1 a2 and a pawn queens.

169) 1 ♘f5! wins at once as 1 ... exf5, 1 ... ♕xf5 and 1 ... ♗xa3 are all met by 2 ♖d8 mate.

170) 1 ♕d2! ♕c5 (1 ... ♕xd2 2 ♖xe7 mate) 2 ♖xe7+ ♕xe7 3 ♕xd5+ ♕e6 4 ♕b7+! and 5 ♕xa8+.

171) 1 ... ♕g3! and if 2 ♖xf1 ♕xg2 mate. If 2 ♘6g4 (or 2 ♘2g4) 2 ... ♕h2+! 3 ♘xh2 ♘g3 mate.

172) 1 ... ♘xf2+! 2 ♖xf2 ♗g2+ 3 ♖xg2 ♖e1+ mating.

173) 1 ♕xh6+! ♗xh6 2 ♖xh6+ ♔g7 3 ♖h7+ ♔f8 4 ♖h8+ ♔g7 5 ♖g8+ ♔h6 6 ♘f7+ ♖xf7 7 g5 mate.

174) 1 ♗b7+! ♕xb7 2 ♕e8+ ♔a7 3 ♗d4+ ♔a6 4 ♕a4 mate.

175) 1 ♖xe5! ♕xf6 (1 ... dxe5 2 ♕c5 mate) 2 ♖e8+, winning.

176) 1 ... ♖de7 2 ♖ae1 (the only way to save the knight) 2 ... ♘xd3 3 ♖d1 ♖xe6 winning a piece, as 4 ♖xe6 ♖xe6 5 ♖xd3 allows 5 ... ♖e1 mate.

177) 1 ♗f5! ♘xf5 (1 ... ♕xf5 2 ♘d6+) 2 ♘f6+ ♔f8 3 ♕e8 mate.

178) 1 ... ♘f2+! 2 ♖xf2 (2 ♔g1 ♘e4+) 2 ... ♗d4! 3 ♕xd4 ♖e1+.

179) 1 ♖e7! ♕xe7 2 ♕d5+ or 1 ... ♘ (or ♗) xe7 2 ♕f7 mate.

180) 1 ♖h8+! ♔xh8 2 ♖xc8+! ♖xc8 3 ♕h3+ ♔g8 4 ♕xc8+ ♔f8 5 ♕e6+ ♔h8 6 ♕h3+ and 7 ♕h7 mate.

Now turn to page 110 to mark down your score.

Chapter Ten

181) This problem is from the game Hassapis – Watson, Harry Baines Memorial British Chess Championships 1990. Black is a piece up and will win eventually, but how can he force an immediate, elegant win?

182) This position is from the game Cavendish – Marsh, Harry Baines Memorial British Chess Championships 1990. Can you spot White's immediate win?

183) This position is from the game Gelfand - Aseev, USSR 1988. Black has a cunning way to win material. Can you see it?

184) This position is from the game Weltmander - Polugayevsky, USSR 1958. Black seems to be in trouble as his knight is pinned and under attack. How does he turn the tables with a tactical sequence?

185) This position is from the game Dolmatov - Kholmov, Sochi 1988. How can White conclude his attack most efficiently.

186) This position is from the game Lautier – J. Polgar, Haifa 1989. In this battle of the two prodigies, White played 1 ♕g5, overlooking a chance to win material in brilliant fashion. Can you see what he missed?

187) This position is from the game Capablanca – Vilaro, Simultaneous, Barcelona 1935. White to play and win.

188) This position is from the game Lazard – Gibaud, Paris 1909. White to play and win.

189) This position is from the game Zaitsev - Nikolaevsky, USSR 1968. How can White conclude his attack most efficiently.

190) This position is from the game Riemann - Kruger, Leipzig 1933. White to play and win

191) This problem is from the game Dzhandzhava - Chandler, Lloyds Bank Masters, London 1990. How can Black finish the game immediately?

192) This position is from the game Adams – Conquest, Lloyds Bank Masters, London 1990. How did White terminate Black's resistance?

193) This position is from the game Short – Nikolic, Tilburg Interpolis International 1990. White, a rook down, looks to be in trouble here. How did he escape his difficulties by forcing a neat draw?

194) This position is from the game Estrin – Rudensky, USSR 1947. White to play and win.

195) This position is from the game Pines – Gabis, USSR 1955. How did Black exploit the awkward placement of the white king?

196) This position is from the game Bauer – Golner, Berlin 1936. Can you spot White's powerful winning combination?

197) This problem is a possibility which was overlooked by the then World Champion Anatoly Karpov. In the game Karpov – Hubner, Montreal 1979, White missed the chance to force this position. Can you see White's knock-out blow?

198) This position is from the game Kosten - Berg, Naestved 1988. The black king has been forced into a dangerous position. Can you see how White finishes off?

199) This position is from the game Kuijf - Rogers, Groningen 1990. How did White force a decisive material gain?

200) This position is from the game de Firmian - Lautier, Bienne 1990. Both rooks are under attack, but it is White's move. Can he do better than capturing Black's rook?

Solutions

181) 1 ... ♗xb2+! 2 ♖xb2 ♕f1+! mating.

182) 1 ♖e7! ♕xe7 2 ♕d3+ ♔h8 (2 ... ♔h6 3 ♕g6 mate) 3 ♘g6+ forcing mate.

183) 1 ... ♗g4! 2 ♖xd6 ♗xf3+ 3 ♖g2 ♗xg2+ 4 ♔g1 ♖xd6 5 ♔xg2 and a rook for knight up, Black wins easily.

184) 1 ... ♘g3+! 2 fxg3 ♕f6+ 3 ♕f2 ♖xe1+ 4 ♔xe1 ♕xf2+ 5 ♔xf2 c2 and the pawn promotes.

185) 1 ♖xh6! ♔xh6 2 ♕h4+ ♔g7 3 ♗xg5 and, after the black queen moves, 4 ♗f6+ and 5 ♕h8 mate follow.

186) 1 ♕e8+ ♔c7 2 ♕xa8! ♗xa8 3 h3! trapping the black queen, when White has a winning advantage.

187) 1 ♖h3+ ♔g4 2 ♔g2 ♖c2 3 ♗h5+ ♔f5 4 ♖f3+ ♔e4 5 ♗g6.

188) 1 ♕xf6+! ♔xf6 2 ♗c3+ mating.

189) 1 ♕xh7+! ♔xh7 2 ♖h3+ ♔g7 3 ♗e7 mate.

190) 1 ♕xg7+! ♔xg7 2 ♗e5+ ♔g8 3 ♘h6 mate.

191) 1 ... ♕xd5! 2 exd5 ♖e1+ 3 ♔g2 ♗f1+ and 4 ... ♗h3 mate.

192) 1 ♖xe4! ♕xe4 2 ♗xf6+! ♗xf6 3 f8(♕) mate.

193) 1 ♕c8+ ♗f8 2 ♕g4+ ♔h8 3 ♕c8! ♔g8 (or 3 ... ♔g7) 4 ♕g4+ with perpetual check.

194) 1 ♕a6! bxa6 2 ♖b8 mate.

195) 1 ... ♖xh3! wins, e.g. 2 ♖xh3 ♖c4, 2 ♖xc7 ♖b3 mate, or 2 ♖fc2 ♖c4+! 3 ♖xc4 ♖b3 mate.

196) 1 ♖xh6+! gxh6 2 ♕g8+ ♘xg8 3 ♗f5 mate. If 1 ... ♔xh6 then 2 ♕g5+ ♔h7 3 ♕h4+ ♔g6 4 f4 is mate.

197) 1 ♖h8+! ♔xh8 2 ♕xh6+ ♕h7 3 ♕f8+ mating.

198) 1 ♘xf5+! gxf5 2 ♖e6+! fxe6 3 ♕f6 mate.

199) 1 ♕d8+! ♗xd8 2 ♖xd8+ ♔f7 3 ♘fg5+ ♖xg5 4 ♘xg5+ and 5 ♘xh3 wins easily.

200) 1 ♗c6! ♖e1+ 2 ♔g2 ♔f8 (to avoid a deadly discovered check) 3 ♖a7! ♗c8 4 ♖a8 wins the bishop.

Now turn to page 110 to mark down your score.

Chapter Eleven

201) This position is from the game Paglilla - Carbone, Argentina 1985. In this tricky position, the black queen is attacked, but White is threatened with a back rank mate. Can you see how White resolves the problem in his favour?

202) This position is from the game Kristev - Tringov, Skopje 1961. Black to play and win.

203) This position is from the game Sznapik - Bernard, Poznan 1971. Although a piece down, White has a tremendously active position. Can you see how he breaks through?

204) This position is from the game Samisch - Ahues, Hamburg 1946. White would like to play 1 f6, but this is met by 1 ... ♛c5+ exchanging queens. How can he improve on this?

205) This problem is from the game Ivanovsky - Lyustrov, Moscow 1972. Black to play and win.

206) This position is from the game Morin – Alain, Montreal 1983. Black has tremendous pressure against the white king position. Can you see how he breaks through?

207) This position is taken from the game Gufeld – Plaskett, Foreign & Colonial Hastings Premier 1986/87. Can you see how White won quickly?

208) This position from the game Larsen – Large, Foreign & Colonial Hastings Premier 1986/87. How did Grandmaster Bent Larsen break through Black's defences here?

209) This position is from the game Larsen - Chandler, Foreign & Colonial Hastings Premier 1987/88. How did Grandmaster Bent Larsen force a swift mate?

210) This position is a variation from the game Smyslov - Kosten, Foreign & Colonial Hastings Premier 1988/89. How can Black force a quick checkmate?

211) This position is from the game Bibby - Basman, Harry Baines Memorial British Chess Championships 1990. Although Black is lacking development, he has a chance to exploit the exposed position of the white king. Can you see it?

212) This position is from the game Cooper – Muir, Harry Baines Memorial British Chess Championships 1990. Black to play and win.

213) This position is from the game Conquest – Hodgson, Lloyds Bank Masters, London 1990. Here, White found a neat way to gain a decisive material advantage. Can you see it?

214) This position is from the game Adams – Suba, Lloyds Bank Masters, London 1990. White has sacrificed a piece for a dangerous attack. Can you see how he continued?

215) This position is from the game Euwe – Keres, Moscow 1948. Black to play and win.

216) This position is from the game Hever – Siklaj, Hungary 1975. Despite the reduced material in this position, White has a mating combination. Can you spot it?

217) This position is from the game Rutherford – Chapman, Brighton 1990. Can you see White's brilliant winning coup?

218) This position is from the game Houghton – Leanse, Hampstead 1990. Black has sacrificed a rook for three pawns and a dangerous attack. How does he continue?

219) This position is from the game Plaskett – Ward, Foreign & Colonial Hastings Challengers 1989/90. Can you see how Black wins immediately?

220) This position is from the game Flear – Emms, Foreign & Colonial Hastings Challengers 1989/90, How does White use the cluster of pieces he has around the black king to force a decision?

Solutions

201) 1 ♕a8! wins, e.g. 1 ... ♖xa8 2 fxe7 and 3 ♖d8.

202) 1 ... ♕h1+! 2 ♔xh1 ♖xh3++ 3 ♔g1 ♖h1 mate.

203) 1 ♖d8! ♖xd8 (1 ... ♗g7 2 ♖b7 mate) 2 c7+ and 3 cxd8(♕) with a winning material advantage.

204) 1 ♖e5! ♗xe5 2 f6 forcing mate.

205) 1 ... ♕d3+! 2 ♖xd3 ♘e1 mate.

206) 1 ... ♘e4! 2 ♗xe4 (2 fxe4 is met the same way) 2 ... ♕xb2+! 3 ♗xb2 ♗xb2 mate.

207) 1 ♖xe8+! ♔xe8 2 ♘c7+ winning the black queen.

208) 1 ♖xf7! ♖xf7 2 ♖d8+ forces mate.

209) 1 ♘f4+! ♔xg4 2 ♗f3 mate.

210) 1 ... ♕xh4+ 2 gxh4 ♖h3 mate.

211) Black wins material after 1 ... a4! 2 ♗c4 d5! threatening the bishop and 3 ... ♗g4 winning the queen.

212) 1 ... ♖c8! 2 ♕xa5 ♖xc1 mate.

213) White broke through with 1 ♖xe7! ♕xe7 2 ♘xg6+ ♖xg6 3 ♕xe7 with a decisive material gain.

214) 1 ♕xe5! ♗xe5 (the same continuation follows after 1 ... dxe5) 2 ♘e6+ and 3 ♘xc7 emerging with two extra pawns.

215) 1 ... ♖xc1! wins, e.g. 2 ♕xc1 ♕xg2 mate or 2 ♖xc1 ♘f3+ and 3 ... ♘xd2.

216) 1 ♖xf7+ ♗xf7 2 ♘f5+ ♔e6 (2 ... ♔e8 3 ♖d8 mate) 3 ♘g7+ ♔e7 4 ♗d8 mate.

217) 1 ♗xg6 ♕xb3 (otherwise Black loses the queen, e.g. 1 ... ♕d5 2 ♗e4+) 2 ♗xh7++! ♔xh7 3 ♖h5 mate.

218) 1 ... ♕g2+! 2 ♕xg2 fxg2+ 3 ♔xg2 ♘e3+ regaining the rook with an easy win.

219) 1 ... ♖xd7 wins. If 2 ♖xd7 ♕g1+.

220) 1 b8(♕)+! ♗xb8 2 ♘b7+ ♔c8 3 ♘e7 mate.

Now turn to page 111 to mark down your score.

Chapter Twelve

221) This problem is from the game Hanov – Ball, USSR 1951. Can you see how White wins immediately?

222) In this position, from the game Pirc – Byrne R, Helsinki 1952, can you see how Byrne spotted an opportunity to cash in on his dangerous pawn on f2?

223) This position is from the game Werner – Webster, Oakham Junior International 1990. Black has just played his rook from b1 to h1. Is this a winning move?

224) Arakhamia – Mortazavi, Oakham Junior International 1990. White to play and win.

225) This position is from the game Levitt – Tisdall, Watson, Farley & Williams International 1990. White to play and win.

Chapter Twelve

226) This position is a possible variation from a game between two English internationals, Hebden - Hodgson, Watson, Farley & Williams International 1990. How can Black exploit the draughty position of the white king?

227) This problem is from the game Semjonov - Loginov, USSR 1952 Can you see how White wins immediately?

228) In this position, from the game Alekhine - Lougovski, Belgrade 1931, can you see how White wins immediately?

229) This position is from the game Bulan – Petrov, USSR 1962. The white king is dangerously restricted. Can you see how Black can exploit this?

230) This problem is from the game Keene – Mestel, Esbjerg 1981. White is threatened with mate, but can you see how he forces an immediate win of material?

231) This position is from the game Kennedy – Davey, *The Times* British Schools Championship 3rd place play-off 1990. How can Black force an immediate win of material?

232) This position is from the game Strens – Maxwell, *The Times* British Schools Championship 3rd place play-off 1990. How did Black capture a vital pawn?

233) In this position, from the game Yusupov – Gulko, Foreign & Colonial Hastings Premier 1989/90, White was on the receiving end of a fine attack. Can you see how the White resistance can be ended here?

234) This position is a variation from the game Sorensen – Plaskett, Foreign & Colonial Hastings Challengers 1989/90. How can White force a quick decision?

235) This position is from the game Kamsky – Gelfand, Tilburg Interpolis International 1990. How did White respond to the challenge to his bishop?

236) This position is from the game Timman – Short, Tilburg Interpolis International 1990. Here White finished off with a classic combination – a rarity in contemporary grandmaster chess. Can you spot it?

237) This position is from the game Mestel – Norwood, Harry Baines Memorial British Chess Championships 1990. How does White exploit his big lead in development?

238) This position is from the game Sadler – Lewis, Harry Baines Memorial British Chess Championships 1990. Black to play and win.

239) This problem is from the game Speelman – Korchnoi, Reykjavik 1988. How can White finish the game immediately?

240) This problem is from the game Boey – Filip, Schilde 1972. How can White make use of his passed pawn?

Solutions

221) 1 ♕xh7+! ♗xh7 2 ♘f7 mate.

222) 1 ... ♖xc3+! 2 ♔xc3 ♘e3 3 ♖xf2 ♘d1+ picks off the black rook.

223) No. After 2 ♖xb2! ♖h2+ 3 ♔f3, Black cannot play 3 ... ♖xb2 as this results in a draw by stalemate.

224) 1 ♘xf5+! gxf5 2 ♖d6+ ♔g7 3 ♖g1+ and 4 ♖g8 mate.

225) 1 ♕xf8+! ♔xf8 2 ♖g8+ ♔f7 3 ♖xd8 and with a rook against a knight, White wins easily.

226) 1 ... ♗xd5! 2 ♖xd5 (2 ♘xd5 ♕xe2) 2 ... ♕a1+! 3 ♔xa1 ♖c1 mate.

227) 1 ♕f6+! ♗xf6 2 ♘f7 mate.

228) 1 ♘e6+! ♘xe6 (1 ... ♗xe6 or 1 ...fxe6 then 2 ♕e7+ and 3 ♕e8 mate) 2 ♕e7+ ♔g8 3 ♕e8+ ♘f8 4 ♘e7 mate.

229) 1 ... ♗xb3+! 2 axb3 ♕c1+! 3 ♖xc1 ♖d2 mate.

230) 1 ♖xe5+! ♗xe5 2 ♘f6+ wins the black queen.

231) 1 ... ♖ae8 wins material – White cannot guard both his rooks.

232) 1 ... ♕xf3 wins a pawn as 2 gxf3 ♗xf3 is mate.

233) 1 ... ♗xg2! 2 ♕xg2 ♖g3 wins the queen. Alternatively 2 ♔xg2 ♖g3+ 3 ♔f2 ♕h2+ 4 ♔e1 ♖e3+ forcing mate.

234) 1 ♖g5! ♕xe4 2 ♖xg7+ ♔f8 3 ♕a3+ ♔e8 4 ♖e1 wins.

235) 1 ♘e4! ♗xh6 2 ♘xd6+ and 3 ♘xb7 winning a crucial pawn.

236) 1 ♘f7+ ♔g8 2 ♘h6++ ♔h8 3 ♕g8+ ♖xg8 4 ♘f7 mate.

237) 1 ♖e7! hxg5 (or f7 caves in) 2 ♕xg5 (threatening 3 ♕xg6+) 2 ... ♔g8 3 ♗xg6 with a swift mate.

238) 1 ... ♘d3+ 2 ♔d1 (2 ♔e2 ♘gf4+ and 3 ... ♖c1 mate; 2 ♔f1 ♖xd2 winning) 2 ... ♖c1+ 3 ♔e2 ♘fg4 mate.

239) 1 ♗e6! and White will emerge a rook for bishop up.

240) 1 ♖d8! ♔xd8 2 h7 and the pawn promotes.

Now turn to page 111 to mark down your score.

Scorechart

The reader who wishes to keep track of his or her progress should record their scores on the following pages. The scoring system is repeated below.

A correct solution in one minute or less: 5 points
A correct solution in two to five minutes: 4 points
A correct solution in six to ten minutes: 3 points
A correct solution in eleven to twenty minutes: 2 points
A correct solution in more than twenty minutes: 1 points

Totals for each chapter:

100 points	Grandmaster
90+ points	International Master
80+ points	Master
70+ points	Expert
60+ points	Strong County Player
50+ points	League Player
40+ points	Club Player
30+ points	Enthusiastic Amateur
20+ points	Social Player
less than 20 points	Read *The Times* every day for regular practice.

Scorechart

Position 1	..... pts	Position 21	..... pts
Position 2	..... pts	Position 22	..... pts
Position 3	..... pts	Position 23	..... pts
Position 4	..... pts	Position 24	..... pts
Position 5	..... pts	Position 25	..... pts
Position 6	..... pts	Position 26	..... pts
Position 7	..... pts	Position 27	..... pts
Position 8	..... pts	Position 28	..... pts
Position 9	..... pts	Position 29	..... pts
Position 10	..... pts	Position 30	..... pts
Position 11	..... pts	Position 31	..... pts
Position 12	..... pts	Position 32	..... pts
Position 13	..... pts	Position 33	..... pts
Position 14	..... pts	Position 34	..... pts
Position 15	..... pts	Position 35	..... pts
Position 16	..... pts	Position 36	..... pts
Position 17	..... pts	Position 37	..... pts
Position 18	..... pts	Position 38	..... pts
Position 19	..... pts	Position 39	..... pts
Position 20	..... pts	Position 40	..... pts

Total for
Chapter 1   ..... pts

Total for
Chapter 2   ..... pts

Scorechart

Position 41	. . . . . pts	Position 61	. . . . . pts
Position 42	. . . . . pts	Position 62	. . . . . pts
Position 43	. . . . . pts	Position 63	. . . . . pts
Position 44	. . . . . pts	Position 64	. . . . . pts
Position 45	. . . . . pts	Position 65	. . . . . pts
Position 46	. . . . . pts	Position 66	. . . . . pts
Position 47	. . . . . pts	Position 67	. . . . . pts
Position 48	. . . . . pts	Position 68	. . . . . pts
Position 49	. . . . . pts	Position 69	. . . . . pts
Position 50	. . . . . pts	Position 70	. . . . . pts
Position 51	. . . . . pts	Position 71	. . . . . pts
Position 52	. . . . . pts	Position 72	. . . . . pts
Position 53	. . . . . pts	Position 73	. . . . . pts
Position 54	. . . . . pts	Position 74	. . . . . pts
Position 55	. . . . . pts	Position 75	. . . . . pts
Position 56	. . . . . pts	Position 76	. . . . . pts
Position 57	. . . . . pts	Position 77	. . . . . pts
Position 58	. . . . . pts	Position 78	. . . . . pts
Position 59	. . . . . pts	Position 79	. . . . . pts
Position 60	. . . . . pts	Position 80	. . . . . pts

Total for		Total for	
Chapter 3	. . . . . pts	Chapter 4	. . . . . pts

Scorechart

Position 81	. . . . . pts	Position 101	. . . . . pts
Position 82	. . . . . pts	Position 102	. . . . . pts
Position 83	. . . . . pts	Position 103	. . . . . pts
Position 84	. . . . . pts	Position 104	. . . . . pts
Position 85	. . . . . pts	Position 105	. . . . . pts
Position 86	. . . . . pts	Position 106	. . . . . pts
Position 87	. . . . . pts	Position 107	. . . . . pts
Position 88	. . . . . pts	Position 108	. . . . . pts
Position 89	. . . . . pts	Position 109	. . . . . pts
Position 90	. . . . . pts	Position 110	. . . . . pts
Position 91	. . . . . pts	Position 111	. . . . . pts
Position 92	. . . . . pts	Position 112	. . . . . pts
Position 93	. . . . . pts	Position 113	. . . . . pts
Position 94	. . . . . pts	Position 114	. . . . . pts
Position 95	. . . . . pts	Position 115	. . . . . pts
Position 96	. . . . . pts	Position 116	. . . . . pts
Position 97	. . . . . pts	Position 117	. . . . . pts
Position 98	. . . . . pts	Position 118	. . . . . pts
Position 99	. . . . . pts	Position 119	. . . . . pts
Position 100	. . . . . pts	Position 120	. . . . . pts

Total for
Chapter 5   . . . . . pts

Total for
Chapter 6   . . . . . pts

Scorechart

Position 121 . . . . . pts	Position 141 . . . . . pts
Position 122 . . . . . pts	Position 142 . . . . . pts
Position 123 . . . . . pts	Position 143 . . . . . pts
Position 124 . . . . . pts	Position 144 . . . . . pts
Position 125 . . . . . pts	Position 145 . . . . . pts
Position 126 . . . . . pts	Position 146 . . . . . pts
Position 127 . . . . . pts	Position 147 . . . . . pts
Position 128 . . . . . pts	Position 148 . . . . . pts
Position 129 . . . . . pts	Position 149 . . . . . pts
Position 130 . . . . . pts	Position 150 . . . . . pts
Position 131 . . . . . pts	Position 151 . . . . . pts
Position 132 . . . . . pts	Position 152 . . . . . pts
Position 133 . . . . . pts	Position 153 . . . . . pts
Position 134 . . . . . pts	Position 154 . . . . . pts
Position 135 . . . . . pts	Position 155 . . . . . pts
Position 136 . . . . . pts	Position 156 . . . . . pts
Position 137 . . . . . pts	Position 157 . . . . . pts
Position 138 . . . . . pts	Position 158 . . . . . pts
Position 139 . . . . . pts	Position 159 . . . . . pts
Position 140 . . . . . pts	Position 160 . . . . . pts

Total for
Chapter 7 . . . . . pts

Total for
Chapter 8 . . . . . pts

Scorechart

Position 161	. . . . . pts	Position 181	. . . . . pts
Position 162	. . . . . pts	Position 182	. . . . . pts
Position 163	. . . . . pts	Position 183	. . . . . pts
Position 164	. . . . . pts	Position 184	. . . . . pts
Position 165	. . . . . pts	Position 185	. . . . . pts
Position 166	. . . . . pts	Position 186	. . . . . pts
Position 167	. . . . . pts	Position 187	. . . . . pts
Position 168	. . . . . pts	Position 188	. . . . . pts
Position 169	. . . . . pts	Position 189	. . . . . pts
Position 170	. . . . . pts	Position 190	. . . . . pts
Position 171	. . . . . pts	Position 191	. . . . . pts
Position 172	. . . . . pts	Position 192	. . . . . pts
Position 173	. . . . . pts	Position 193	. . . . . pts
Position 174	. . . . . pts	Position 194	. . . . . pts
Position 175	. . . . . pts	Position 195	. . . . . pts
Position 176	. . . . . pts	Position 196	. . . . . pts
Position 177	. . . . . pts	Position 197	. . . . . pts
Position 178	. . . . . pts	Position 198	. . . . . pts
Position 179	. . . . . pts	Position 199	. . . . . pts
Position 180	. . . . . pts	Position 200	. . . . . pts

Total for
Chapter 9   . . . . . pts

Total for
Chapter 10   . . . . . pts

Scorechart

Position 201 ..... pts	Position 221 ..... pts
Position 202 ..... pts	Position 222 ..... pts
Position 203 ..... pts	Position 223 ..... pts
Position 204 ..... pts	Position 224 ..... pts
Position 205 ..... pts	Position 225 ..... pts
Position 206 ..... pts	Position 226 ..... pts
Position 207 ..... pts	Position 227 ..... pts
Position 208 ..... pts	Position 228 ..... pts
Position 209 ..... pts	Position 229 ..... pts
Position 210 ..... pts	Position 230 ..... pts
Position 211 ..... pts	Position 231 ..... pts
Position 212 ..... pts	Position 232 ..... pts
Position 213 ..... pts	Position 233 ..... pts
Position 214 ..... pts	Position 234 ..... pts
Position 215 ..... pts	Position 235 ..... pts
Position 216 ..... pts	Position 236 ..... pts
Position 217 ..... pts	Position 237 ..... pts
Position 218 ..... pts	Position 238 ..... pts
Position 219 ..... pts	Position 239 ..... pts
Position 220 ..... pts	Position 240 ..... pts

Total for
Chapter 11   ..... pts

Total for
Chapter 12   ..... pts